Free Verse Editions

Edited by Jon Thompson

ALIAS

PROSE POEMS

Eric Pankey

Parlor Press
Anderson, South Carolina
www.parlorpress.com

Parlor Press LLC, Anderson, South Carolina, 29621

Library of Congress Cataloging-in-Publication Data on File

978-1-64317-140-1 (paperback)
978-1-64317-141-8 (pdf)
978-1-64317-142-5 (ePub)

1 2 3 4 5

Cover art: "Brothers," Lars Elling, by kind and generous permission of the artist, http://www.larselling.no

Parlor Press, LLC is an independent publisher of scholarly and trade titles in print and multimedia formats. This book is available in paperback and ebook formats from Parlor Press on the World Wide Web at http://www.parlorpress.com or through online and brick-and-mortar bookstores. For submission information or to find out about Parlor Press publications, write to Parlor Press, 3015 Brackenberry Drive, Anderson, South Carolina, 29621, or email editor@parlorpress.com.

for Marvin Bell

forgetfulness is never complete
—Jean Follain

. . .can you tell me where we're headin'?
Lincoln County Road or Armageddon?
—Bob Dylan

Contents

Contents

Alias

I.

Alias

Like everyone he passed on the street, he entered the world nameless. Names attached themselves to him: José, Albert, Cornelius, Jake, Tyrone, Soren. . . . He wore each easily like a well-tailored coat. He would take it off at night, place it upon a hanger, and in the morning emerge with a new name from the closet. The names multiplied. His lovers each with his or her own endearment: My Lamb, Little Neptune, Sugar Pie, Pale Ramon. . . . And the children at the bus stop, who called out tauntingly, Uncle or Boo or Señor Zoobeck. Recognized, he would tip his hat. To some, he was a mail carrier. To some, a bookie. To some, he was the dapper pensioner, ivory-handled cane in hand, who strolled each evening around the plaza in Vejer de la Frontera. To some, he was the last of the Czar's tragic family. *I* could not stand in for his many heteronyms, but *I* is what he called himself at night in his prayers to God, as he had as a boy, at that time, still nameless—unmoored, anchorless, adrift—a pronoun without an antecedent.

II.

Et in Arcadia Ego

Wherever the tent is set down and unfolded, within it one finds a sacred precinct, the archaic pent up in a panpipe's scale, bees heavy amid the hexagons' viscous gold. Beneath this shelter of a capital *A*, one is offered a Neolithic hunter's amber bear amulet, a palm leaf as a figure for a swan.

Exercise in Intuition

To render Time sensible is itself the task.

—Gilles Deleuze

The past is inaccessible, archived on some obsolete technology. Overhead, the hourglass's emptying orb. Overhead, an ocean of black gall.

Delacroix paints things lit by the half-light of a gray day. Leonardo notes the tendency of colors to move toward blue-gray as they recede from the eye.

Is it more nostalgic to restore the ruin to its original state, or to hope the ruin's current broken-down condition is preserved?

Verdigris gathers on the toppled slabs—still dark with last night's rain—of gravestones.

Osage oranges, which I called as a child *hedge apples*, are of the mulberry family. I am plagued with what Freud calls "the symptom of 'being conscious.'"

The low light of the subsequent night long exposure reveals *the-not-apparent*. Instinct, by its nature, is archaic. Each thought is ahead of itself and too late.

The Apprenticeship

In the end, what could the boy do? He liked to play with matches, to close the cover and strike, to watch the spark turn inward, crackle, then flare, sometimes straight up into a flame, other times and, only for an instant, into a helix that unspiraled into a fiery teardrop. Sometimes, the matches, soft with humidity, bent and tore and would not catch. He apprenticed himself to fire. Heraclitus says, *All things are an exchange for fire and fire for all things.* The boy braided fuses out of rags, knew the after-mark of each accelerant, held his palm open above the candle longer than was needed, read biographies of the great arsonists. Jesus says, *I came to set fire to the world, and I wish it were already burning.* Bob Dylan sings, *You can play with fire, but you'll get the bill.*

Post-Diluvian

The water subsided. The clouds broke up. Little would burn after the deluge. Fires sputtered and quenched themselves. Cows, goats, whole flocks of birds—unscavenged, bloated—cluttered the fields like scattered erratics. How quiet it was without the rain pelting the shoreless distance, without the constant company of thunder.

I gleaned a message from randomness, called it *the new covenant.*

With only a bundle of notebooks as a pillow, I lay my head down.

Outtakes from *The Newlywed Game*

In the crowd around the victim, she is the one who admonishes: Give this poor person room to breathe. He prefers a tender touch to an apology. She thinks he is the one who should apologize. They first met, he says, because he sensed the gaze of an unknown viewer. They met, she says, because she had always wanted to be a contestant on *The Newlywed Game*. She insists that none of the resurrection sightings are authentic, but are a manifestation of a group hallucination that moved like a contagion among Jesus' followers in their grief. Noted, he responds, noting in his daybook yet another non sequitur on her part. Regarding *making whoopie*, she compares it to an algorithm that collapses into randomness. He compares it to the water's surface: fugitive, ethereal, a depth without reflection. She shakes her head *no* and says, you mean it is like a fog illumined from within, aglow yet opaque. Yeah, he says. What she said.

What Is the Purpose of Your Visit?

To attend an uncle's funeral. To have a boil lanced. To return an overdue library book. To track the Nile back to its source. To turn myself in. To seek asylum. To take monastic vows. To party. To destabilize the government. To see Paris in springtime. To escape a bad marriage. To claim lottery winnings. To take hostages. To negotiate the release of hostages. To restore a fresco. To catch a glimpse of the coronation. To evangelize. To see again Turner's "Rough Sea with Wreckage." To cut down a paratrooper caught in the highest branches. To donate a kidney. To experience firsthand a state of emergency. To use frequent flyer miles before they expire.

Prospero in Exile

Wedded to the past, he is a passer-by. How to distinguish between a *pain put upon* and a *pain extracted from*? On the shortwave: voices, but none speaks a language he can translate. Nevertheless he listens and is kept company, surrounded in his solitude. Wind shuffles chaff off the threshing floor, but the fog stays put. Its hem: wet raw linen. Sounds enlarge and amplify: a ship's stuttering engine, gull squabble, a rope snagged on a squeaking pulley. The signal fire burned out long ago. Come nightfall, he'll enter easily, willingly, the exile of sleep.

The Late Shift

for Mark Strand

This is the hour of fireflies, of Venus as bright as a tiepin on raw silk. This is the hour when a fox and her kits disappear beneath a house propped up on jacks, when ten thousand bats spiral from a cracked rockface, swirl and swoop and veer away. This is the hour that slips like a bead from a rosary. This is the hour a janitor nudges ahead of himself with a push broom: each minute bristles with static; each second, like a dropped crystal, divides into a thousand versions of itself. This is the hour when *magic,* under various names, flourishes, when from the molten core, magma rises and an island is born, when archipelagos sprout from the writhing waters like seeds from a dark furrow. This is the hour when sleep is the only shortcut to morning. This is the hour a barn owl returns, roosts in the church's charred rafters.

The Other Story About José

after Carlos Drummond de Andrade

Jill, hoping to spice things up, suggests to her husband, Kevin, that they invite Helen to join them for a threesome. Helen, while flattered, feels such an appeal from her immediate supervisor inappropriate and reports Jill to the Office of Equity and Diversity Services. Ted, a senior manager at the Office of Equity and Diversity Services, is asked to investigate the charge and finds, much to his dismay, that he is infatuated with Jill, and although she is fired, he finds ways to continue to bump into her. He begins to attend her church. Ted works with Kevin, Jill's husband, decorating the church for Advent. As they are hanging the Christmas greens, Ted confesses to Kevin his love for Jill, and Kevin, surprised by the revelation, loses his footing and falls from the ladder onto the sanctuary's hardwood floor. Kevin dies. Helen, feeling double remorse for getting Jill fired and, by a direct chain of events, Kevin killed, attends the funeral. Before the night is over, Helen admits to Jill that the only reason she did not join in the threesome was the third party, Kevin. Helen admits her desire for Jill and they go home that night together, surprised at the fervor of their newfound love. Ted, who continues to stalk Jill, watches through her second story bedroom window as the two women undress. Knowing that the Fates love irony, Ted has asked his friend José to hold the ladder steady, so he—Ted, that is—is not the second man to fall from a ladder in this story. José owes Ted a big favor, thus he stands amid the dark, scratchy shrubbery and holds the ladder. The story of that favor is another story entirely.

After the Rapture

After the unexpected departures, lights still burn in empty rooms. The bare tree leafed-out with starlings still murmurs and stirs past twilight. The commute, less congested, adds another hour of leisure to the day and that hour longer for its aimlessness. When the chosen, ungrounded by gravity, lifted away from the lawns and sidewalks, we had time enough to bid them *bon voyage!* We were neighbors after all and although we rarely talked we had always waved warmly as we hurried through our daily disarray.

To Fix an Image in Memory

The French doors (one cracked open at this hour when I had meant to look out and beyond) offer reflection: a double self-portrait at odd angles with itself as if two men consulted on something they'd prefer I not hear.

Speed Dating

He says, "Sometimes, attended only by my reflection, I squint and feel the drill bit of a headache begin to whir at a low speed behind my right eye, and what I am actually sensing in my peripheral vision is the gravity of interstellar gasses as they flare and contract, condense into a giant planet worthy of a god's name: a ferric atmosphere of rust, lifeless lead at its core, its oceans contending with the orbits of three moons."

"Fair enough," she says, "you're a sensitive guy. But this genre usually begins with a question and not a confession."

Lilith As a Figure for the Moon

Lacking a thread, she unbinds the book she once read aloud by the evening light of lupines, and those words—lead's drab gloam awaiting transformation—seemed as sweet as fresh water pulled into a marsh's estuarial green: a meander inlaid with mirrors, another stratum of twilight gathering.

What had he called her—*night hag? Screech owl?*

He was so good at naming.

The Anvil

Although grass has grown around it, you can see for yourself it is an anvil, there at the edge of the frontier, like some extinct cousin to the rhinoceros: a rough skin of rust on the flat face and on the conical width of the pocked and scored protruding horn. Of course, there is always a gap between the thing and the description of the thing. Dull, heavy, and dense, it waits—an excess of inertia—for the downward stroke. The very use of the anvil, over time, deforms it. A thrush will strike snail shells on stones to get at the flesh. The lithic anvil is replaced by the bronze, the bronze by the wrought iron, the wrought iron by the wrought iron faced with steel. You came here to the edge of the frontier to escape the violence of allegory, the current theorems and fashions, and refuse to see the anvil as an altar. You put your two index fingers, pointing up, next to your temples and pretend to be a bull. The anvil is your unmoved opponent.

False Sermon — True Story

For Michael Palmer

Like it or not, they get our weather tomorrow. Like us, they enter memory, assured it is finite. Tomorrow: winter in its one disguise. Tomorrow: a hitherto purely imagined form. You can toss, if you wish, salt in the fire as an offering. To be safe, you might as well throw in three rose seeds, three nettle seeds, two rue leaves, and three cumin seeds. Crushed cumin will not do. They call the secret poison *spider in the dumpling.* Write down the recipe in your little book of misfortunes, your little book of micrographia. The lacuna's deep taproot (which must not be pulled, but dug up), smells like a beet or a parsnip—sweet and loamy. It is to the tongue what the incantation of a broom is to the ear. Tomorrow. But not before the daily demise of evening. Each brushstroke had a name—*little hatchet, combed-out hemp, serpent's tail, the pulled carpenter's nail*—but they called it *spilled ink,* and went to fetch a mop. All the while forgetting the emptiness that is the site of transformation, the emptiness that is an intermediary. They waste a good deal of time waiting for intuition to flash forth, then fall prey to gloom. They could have called us. The wintery mix arrived here yesterday.

Convalescence

Though subdued, his fever remained. Snow had closed the interstate. He had time to delineate his boredoms, to inspect his thoughts. His mother lifted the cast-iron skillet with two hands, drained bacon fat into a tin can. How easily the morning tired, aged into evening. The fever stayed on like a pilot light. Sleep, a useless pursuit, so easily achieved. Sleep heavy, the weight and depth of lake ice. Thus submerged, he practiced breathing underwater.

III.

The Surveyor's Map

Water sheds south by southeast into a run. The floodplain—boggy, clay-dense—is wide, flanked by trash trees, invasive vines, and thickets. Far off, a dog barks, suggesting, perhaps, a neighbor.

Although the sky is not indicated, it borders all and is displaced as elevation increases.

Habitation

The straight lines of the house—framed-in, but no walls hung—
against the bent back of the sky, compose a habitation of expectancy.
The hours drag and slur, stretch to attach themselves to departure.
Those who might occupy the house have to imagine the outside
kept out, windows to narrow the narrow light, a floor nailed down
board by board above the rain-grayed foundation, the rain swished
away through gutters, down downspouts. The house sits at the sharp
end of a wooded island formed by a river and an anabranch and
as the rain falls through open rafters, the island narrows between
the waters.

To Document the Ephemeral

Consider an immensity of fixed stars, of number numberless. From the vantage point of the present tense, are hours integral elements of a predetermined form or more afterthoughts, haphazard improvisations in the wide field of ether? Consider the bent stem of a parrot tulip on which a dewdrop balances and magnifies a spot of decay. A shabby wonder, its priceless petals fall one by one.

The Unexpected Return

Despite our best efforts, we gave up renaming the constellations, given the confines of speech, nine always turning out to be six, the effort interrupted again by a motion to quash subpoena.

Night spread wide across the island until a dispersing agent spilled from a crop duster. Then it was morning again with unexpected media coverage and roadwork ahead.

It seemed we had crossed an international dateline. All the color in the white angel's trumpet blossoms shivered as *white*. The moon covered the sun, as most are acutely aware.

Sometimes an image arises out of nowhere and its source (an old newsreel? a dream?) escapes us: a group of explorers looks down where the ice thins; the sled dogs, agitated, whimper.

The recollection, however, offers an unexpected return. It seems possible to retranslate the prophecy to benefit not just the rich, to draw the complexity of the ostrich plume ginger as a single continuous line.

By Another Route

One is haunted. Haunted, one must proceed nonetheless with the courtesy of a host. One assumes the ghost is lost and needs to be helped on its way. One sees things others do not see. Or rather one sees things that others cannot see.

One surrenders. Gives in. Is overtaken. Possessed. One learns a new language that one speaks, as one reads, silently. Words given shape in the throat and mouth but not sounded. The experience leaves one short of breath, if not breathless.

How deeply a ghost hungers. It cannot eat. If it could, it would never be sated. Exiled as it is from the past and the future, a ghost resides in the here and now. The hour slows. Hardens. As translucent as amber.

: :

The difference between this world and the next is slight, barely no-
ticeable, what one might call *a flaw in continuity* or *a bad splice*.
There: the wheeze of a concertina. Here: a drain coming unstuck.
One crosses a threshold uninvited. One, invitation in hand, knocks
at the door ajar.

The *uncanny*, Freud says, is *something which ought to have remained
hidden but has come to light*. One can recall the view from the palmist's
window: dim, featureless, but not the fortune read aloud from one's
own hand. The gaze is always introspective: dim and featureless.

Look: the grubby dun of a penumbral nocturne. One descends in
the dark to the cellar to find the fuse box. Another worn set of con-
crete stairs, it seems, around each corner to take one deeper down in
the mountain into which the cellar is dug.

: :

One subtracts everything that is not God and finds a minus sign. One returns to the dog-eared pages and finds little of significance. The marginalia, although cryptic, is in no way noteworthy or evocative. To find one's way, keep the mountain to the right.

Subtracted from the inventory: three thousand hand-carved ivory beads in a Cro-Magnon grave, a sieve to separate out prime numbers, the parabolic path of Holofernes' blood splatter away from Judith's blade, Heisenberg's *formal description of the relations among perceptions* . . .

If sacrifice is necessary, Ai Weiwei says, *it must be accompanied by the appropriate ceremonies, as an unceremonious sacrifice is a crime against the natural world.* One removes layer after layer of the shellac's sulfurous yellow, nonetheless, the painted mountain looks like a dung heap steaming.

: :

The ladder's shadow, more solid than the ladder, holds up the wall. Although the days grow longer, it gets dark early these days. The expected terminus never arrives. The wall leans a little now. One can hear at the base of the falls the water mend its breakage.

Dust alights evenly: a seamless transition. No skirmishes, no scrimmages, no play on words in a room with a single chair and a sign on the door saying: *Space for forgetting*. Here various pasts overlap. A line contains infinite points yet reads as an incomplete sentence.

There is nothing with which the night won't merge: conditional probability, pared-back harmonic distortions, or the vexations of a chance encounter. One can dowse for a single point of light, but find instead latent notions and primal forms. How strange, how other a body.

: :

Objects with an unobstructed line of sight with one another are said to be *intervisible.* One builds a house with sticks. Light and ocean seep through seams and cracks. Sea levels rise. The weight of the land sinks. Nonetheless, the view is uninterrupted.

In Bruegel's "Triumph of Death," a rickety wagon full of skulls passes. Two ships sink in the offing. Death on a reddish horse hauls an oversized scythe into war. In the lower right hand corner, somehow oblivious to the battle, a lutist serenades his beloved.

As in the lightproof box of a camera, or in the depth of a cave, one finds a dark that transcends the absence of light, a dark virtually impenetrable, a dark that warps like an opaque plasma or malleable metal to touch. Then the shutter opens.

: :

In a dream, a yellow snake insinuates itself beneath the foot-worn marble stoop. Each flick of its tongue causes feedback and interference on the kitchen radio. When one pries up the stoop with a crowbar, the snake refuses to budge. Coils tighter.

A mere touch is enough to shimmer a plumb line. A serpent sheds its skin, but a serpent does not emerge—rather a sensation. The sensation of a thought. To liberate the unknown, one exchanges intention for chance. The day, hinged like a book, blows shut in a bluster.

One breathes in and the house fills. When the house is asleep what does the attic dream? A spell loses at last its adhesiveness thus must be spoken again. One breathes in and the house fills. When one breathes out how does the house not collapse?

: :

One comes burdened with maps, almanacs, and field guides. The source of the river is an underworld spring. To drink from it is to drowse, to forget the difference between cause and effect and happenstance, between yesterday and a series of irrational permutations.

(The repose of sleep refreshes only the body, Bachelard says. *It rarely sets the soul at rest. The repose of the night does not belong to us. It is not the possession of our being. Sleep opens within us an inn for phantoms. In the morning we must sweep out the shadows.)*

The stag at the river's edge waits with the ageless confidence of a god. It does not drink—instinct leads the herd to glacier-fed creeks and meadow ponds. One will not recall the errancy, but one recalls the thirst. Having tracked the herd this far, one gives into thirst.

: :

The snow, earthward, is blown high again. Winter rehearses its single line of dialogue. Who can deny the ease of forgetting; deny the barbed precisions of each crystalline flake? Hidden behind gray clouds: a ruined weld of stars.

In the presence of a camera, time hesitates. It's like that moment when the horse breaks into a gallop and one feels oneself untethered from gravity. One is not flying but falling. Call it *what one has known all along.* Call it *the theory of unsupported transit.*

Begin with a footnote. Misalign the syntax as spindrift residue, as what a body transcribes through space: an inherent ephemerality, the flux of a dance enacted, the fixed site of the veering. Begin again. Draw from life as if from memory.

: :

Looking out at the sea, one is far from home. One loses track of the truth, which has the substance of shadow, of a stain that blooms on a wetted surface. A horizontal line makes of emptiness a sky—gray hovers over gray—a record of incremental change.

One acknowledges the duration. One embellishes and mistakes the middle distance for the elsewhere of late afternoon. Looking out at sea, one is far from arresting the image, far from pinpointing the coordinates, far from completing the required reading.

One is far from home and just now beginning to appreciate the scribbled formula left up on the blackboard all semester, to appreciate the Romantic potential of the grid and the way it holds each element in place. Far from home, one loses track of the truth.

: :

One is on a treacherous errand and finds Achilles among the breath-less dead. He tries to speak but cannot. His face is a mirror of the past: blurred and distressed. One registers winter's redundancy as the remainder of a remainder. One takes the rough path up and out.

The night leans in like a reader over a book. The reader's own shadow makes the words dim and barely legible. One is like such a reader, which is to say one is like the night. One settles into read just as the light begins its haggard retreat.

We are surrounded by curtains, Magritte says. *We only perceive the world behind a curtain of semblance. At the same time, an object needs to be covered in order to be recognized at all.* Yes, one can bribe the dead, sacrifice a bird or lamb, let the dead wet their tongues. Yet one has come empty-handed.

: :

With the best of intentions, one refuses to assuage a hankering. One habituates the out-of-sync background noise and hears, at last, a pulse. *Don't jinx it for me*, one begs, but a spell cast cannot be un-cast, only countered by a different spell.

How easily the objects become arrangements of shapes, shadows, and lines. The weather goes about its unmaking. The librettist awaits a collaborator. Awaits the interval, the harmony. *Say uncle*, one is commanded and one gives in, gives up, begs for mercy.

One limits the set of conventions, or limits the colors on the palette to, say, terra rosa, yellow ochre, and cobalt blue, and this, then, be-comes the *form*, the *constraint*, within which and against which one works. As if by a spell, the objects reassert themselves as *objects*.

: :

How to hold in mind all that might be of use: the Nile's flood sched-
ule, for instance, or how often to have the chimney swept? One
keeps one's eye open. The river widens, stretches toward the sea.
Smoke uncoils upward like a length of rope.

If we keep the eyes open, Goethe says, *in a totally dark place, a certain
sense of privation is experienced. The organ is abandoned to itself; it re-
tires into itself.* The soul is dormant—suspended and asleep. Retired
into itself, the eye cannot behold the soul as image or afterimage.

One attempts to fix and chart the ocean, to evaporate seawater to
catalog the mineral residue. One holds one's breath and goes under.
One's eyes adjust. But how to hold one's breath long enough? How
not to float back to the surface?

: :

Furtive, fragile, one awaits a meaningful coincidence. Charcoal vestiges of the underdrawing muddy the clarity of the lead white. It does not take long to lapse into narrative, for the pretext to shear off the text like an iceberg from a glacier. One waits for such a coincidence.

What remains of prior decisions: erased gestures, a fault line visible at the surface. To enact a mirage, one hangs a turmeric-stained square of silk in front of a square of stark, rough white cotton canvas. To enact a monsoon, one waits like everyone else for the rain to fall.

Astray, one continues. One confesses to nostalgia, to the weight of longing. But one is merely guilty of mis-remembering. One sets out in search for the miraculous, but soon settles for trial and error. One had a plan, but returns by another route.

Night Wedding

We repurpose the ungoverned hours as a banquet table. Jerry-rig an aisle to keep separate families and factions. With invisible ink, set a lunar sliver at the sky's far edge. Out of the fog's gray and Lenten hues, a fox bark announces the processional's somber approach. Vows and rings are exchanged. Blessings bestowed. Birdseed we throw falls. Germinates. Lifts as a flock.

From This Day Forward

It's hard to get there from here, what with the detours, and worse, the makeshift memorials and all the rubbernecking. Yet staying put has its cost. The moon—unerasable—stowed in the lake's depth, for example, must be hoisted up by ropes, and rehung nightly above oaks. Let's agree that the gyrfalcon's belled jess gives its prey a little edge, a sporting chance. Let's agree that by their attributes—a jar of ointment, an ax in the head—we recognize the saints.

Honeymoon at the Pine Crest
Motor Hotel and Cabins

You grow sensitive to the slightest sound. Light years away, a star flickers out. You hear the needles click and clack as a spider knits in the corner. In the next town, a car backfires. What is taking her so long in the bathroom? It is not the infinite you fear, but the slow tick of the hour. The only way out of the room: a thin rope of smoke up the chimney. If you could get a grip, you'd shimmy up.

Childhood

Winter arrived: a blunt, blue spectrum of ice. The fog, a milky nimbus, froze and shattered. Three sodden paths converged where a snowman stood. A custodian of the ephemeral, you kept icicles, like spiraled narwhal tusks, in the root cellar among moss and sawdust. When you returned in spring, you found them stolen. The past (even then you knew) was like a scab. Worry it enough and blood will well up to reseal. You liked best in the story where the frail dog, Argos, encounters the old man in disguise. Ten minutes before your father arrived home your own dog would go to the front door and wait.

The Theft

The old woman claims we've stolen her memories. When asked for an example, she will not be fooled and says, *You have them. How should I know?* Even if we had, what would we have? The plots of novels? The diary of a honeymoon where things went awry? Up early, she watches the morning star linger, rebuilds a scaffold of logic to scale the day. Like a newborn, she practices the startle reflex. She forgets she asked us not to return. She believes we are castaways and it's about time someone invented a sundial or a pulley system, or at least learned to empty the dishwasher.

Visiting Your Father at the Hospital

Split by stroke, he will relearn to talk. Will learn to write with his left hand. He leans lopsided, numbness and ghost-pain all along his right side, the dragged deadweight of which catches up with his body's working portion, with which, and against your will, he meets you halfway, embraces you.

The Sleeper

At night, her heart, a barn owl, departs without a sound. She wears a mask of gouged-out wood made moon-bright with gesso. Near where ferns drape a spring, she hunts. Attuned to the *almost-imperceptible,* she hears her own wings in the guise of silence, apprehends her shadow in the dark river bottom, the sequence of corridors within a mazy wood. She wakes where she fell asleep, an interior lit from without, with a fine weather of words on her tongue.

A Story Coalescing

At a party, we keep talking as if we know each other, as if we took part in a screen test for a movie not yet written, not yet financed, an idea really for a scene around which the director imagines a story coalescing. We are to improvise.

I say, "I am not unaware of the claim the past has upon the present."

And you comment on a habit you have of finding anachronisms in novels. It takes me a moment or two to hear this not as a non sequitur, but as an apt rejoinder—curious, insightful.

You ask, "Do you know Paolo Uccello's 'Battle of San Romano?'"

"Of course," I say. "It is my go-to example of single-point perspective when the subject, on occasion, comes up."

"Me too," you say and it seems we have known each other a long time, as the discussion takes on the documentary precision of a dream.

You lean in closer and say under your breath, "To be seen is to know shame."

And I think back on what I said earlier and reply, "No. To *have been* seen is to know shame."

Not Good with Faces

She is not good with faces, which is not to say that all faces look the same to her. On the contrary, each face—distinct, individual— seems familiar, seems like someone she knows or met once, thus she is quick with a *hello* or a *good to see you* to a stranger on the street, who, surprised by kindness, might look puzzled. Or smiles. Or tips a hat. Whichever is the custom where the greeting takes place. In India, or Nepal, say, this person or that in a crowd just might be the tea-seller from the train station, or the helpful conductor from the last leg of the journey. The street sweeper in Paris, who offered her directions, must be, she is now certain, the acrobat's twin brother in the little family circus she paid three euros last night to watch. In the hill town's lower gravel parking lot, the acrobat, now dressed as a laborer, is dismantling the red tent. A goat, which is part of the act, chews something and does not strain at the end of its chain. Straw floats in the water-filled tin bucket next to it. The goat stands still in the mottled shade, unperturbed, and chews. She knows this goat: the blunt horns, the uncanny, hyphen-like pupils, the way it will not meet her eyes.

The Butcher

1. After the floor is mopped with bleach and the counters wiped down, the butcher closes his eyes and imagines he is standing next to an indoor swimming pool at the Holiday Inn in Lincoln, Nebraska.

2. The butcher finds it odd how few kinds of animals he is asked to butcher. Cows, pigs, chickens, lambs—that's his bread and butter. Only now and then a duck or goose at Christmas, a deer or two during hunting season.

3. The butcher does not bring his work home. His wife is a vegetarian.

4. The butcher finds the names of things delicious on his tongue: *a rack of lamb, a brisket, a London broil, a minute steak, a skinless, boneless thigh, a Sunday roaster, a New York strip, corned beef. . . .*

5. A pet peeve: someone who makes no purchase but asks, *A bone for my dog perhaps?*

6. After the floor is mopped with bleach and the counters wiped down and each knife is in its place, the butcher breathes deep and imagines the Holiday Inn's indoor swimming pool; imagines he has driven the six hours to Lincoln to catch a basketball game. His wife has stayed home. She prefers TV to basketball, her own bed to one strangers have slept in.

7. Once making sausage, the butcher thought, *It's like watching sausage being made.* That is an example of what his wife calls dryly "butcher's humor."

The Hyenas

A pair of hyenas stood at the door, dressed not unlike missionaries: black pants, white button-down shirts, their backpacks a little too snug under their armpits.

One said—*We agree with John Cage, art should not be used as self-expression but as self-alteration.*

The other said—*Or consider what René Char said about why he became a writer: A bird's feather on my windowpane in winter and all at once there arose in my heart a battle of embers never to subside again.*

Before I could get a word in edgewise, the one said—quoting I think Gaston Bachelard—*If a poet looks through a microscope or a telescope, he always sees the same thing.*

I had to admit these were some smart hyenas. Yet each time they spoke, their hackles went up and whatever they said felt like a threat. Not to mention the snickering, the tee-hee-ing, the saliva matting their chin hairs.

I stood in the doorframe. I didn't want them entering. I had forgotten whether hyenas are scavengers or predators.

I really have to go—I said, but the one hyena put his paw between the screen and the jamb.

Okay—he said—*but before we go, remember what Horace said—Many brave men lived before Agamemnon; but all are overwhelmed in eternal night, unwept, unknown, because they lack a sacred poet.*

The other hyena, tugging his friend away by a backpack strap, attempting to ease the tension, said to me—*Perhaps you are just that sacred poet.*

IV.

The Return of Odysseus

To gather the evening's cool, the shutters are left open. All at once the cicadas, dumbstruck, cease. She turns toward the shore, senses a squall in the offing. In anticipation of a kiss, she swallows; touches her tongue to her lips. The moon sheds light as transparent as a threadbare dress.

Ariadne on Naxos

The goat bells descend. It must be nightfall. Fireflies, little lamps snuffed and relit, survey the woods' depths. The cloud-fed mosses on the ridge edge grow inky black. Thumb-struck, the match flares brighter, noisier than it ought. She closes her eyes, untangles a maze's abstruse distance into a line.

Circe's Island

She hears a boat far out, its oars' entry; hears the stove's circle of blue flames; hears soup simmer in an uncovered copper kettle. She skips ahead pages in an overwrought novel. Fresh water sleeps in the cool depths of cisterns. A grappling hook pulls the horizon farther out into the fog to some unseen point where waves set out in opposite directions.

Lazarus

He cannot breathe in the dream, tears at the woven cocoon shrouding his face, and thus interrupts the progress and machinery of metamorphosis.

When the ash is raked no live ember is unbanked.

Between Solon and Cedar Rapids on Highway One, 1984

Driving on into the storm I scroll the distance of static between radio stations. Ahead: the shallow, grainy depth headlights cut into sleet. And behind: the winter's painstaking erasures.

Out of whose womb came the ice? the preacher, the single strong signal on the radio, asks. I move—a point on a breadthless length—and stand still. A tunnel opens before me and closes behind.

Elegy with Moonlit Doorway

As a boy, he wandered in dreams down a long portico: archways like cells in an abandoned hive, like the elaborate architecture of marrow.

The moon: a bolus of fur and bones.

Moonlight: a dust of crushed pearls.

Memory cannot keep up and the past piles up outside the door, un-inventoried. He pushes the door open, calls the dog in for the night. Waits a long time before he recalls the dog is dead.

Catalogue Raisonné

The single sentence of the day— an alphabet of bone, keepsakes and meanwhiles— ends as it ought: *period.*

The method, adhered to rigorously, is simple: *repetition following a rule.*

The rule changes, though with subtlety.

It's not as if an oath were broken and a city sacked, or that one could see now without assistance the Cat's Eye Nebula in the constellation Draco.

The shop is closed for inventory.

The blinds are drawn to keep secret the languorous counting.

Midsummer.

Still light out.

Without apprehension we call it *a night.*

Asked to Account for His Whereabouts

He recalls the tumble of coal through a chute, the frost-heaved path stones loose in their muddy sockets, an opossum hiss, lit up by headlights, but cannot distinguish if these are of a single day or of several. The dried reeds, a gold without luster, rustle at the marsh's edge, where once fireworks set the wetland ablaze. He has not a single memory of the fourth grade, or his teacher, Mrs. _____, her name lost. His sixth grade teacher Miss Zanoni, wore a houndstooth wool jumper on picture day, the same one she wore each Friday, with a bell-sleeved white blouse, when she'd read a chapter from a novel—he believes it was called *The Imposter*—aloud, an elaborate tale of espionage and assumed identities. He gets up, still groggy from the general anesthesia, and pulls an IV bottle crashing to the recovery room's waxed linoleum floor. He manages not to cut his feet. Each memory topples into another, his mind a stumble. Asked to account for his whereabouts, where he was between ten p.m and two a.m. on the day in question, he concedes he has no alibi.

Depiction Without a Subject

When the world was flat, we could stand at the edge and take the whole thing in. Windows held a snow-reflected transparency and let light pass through. We recalled the static on the line, but not the conversation. We could not tame time, could not change its velocity or direction. The mysterious immateriality of eternity, it turns out, is a byproduct of nostalgia. Somewhere along the line, the gods fell out of favor. Shameless, we shared an anecdote, a bit of gossip, our memories still intact. We understood the attraction of the *not-quite-complete*: the vertiginous arc of the story we told and in telling came to believe.

A Slipknot as It Slips

Escape the body for a while. Escape from the tired flesh, from doorways and mirrors where shadows brood. Slip like a snake from your skin into an ever-new raw glare. Give in. Let the past and the eternal vie for significance. You are a blank page in a census book, the elegant straight line of a censor's cross out, the senseless and the clandestine, a little frenzy of wind. Slip the snare of birth, the unruly moment of perception, the grids and systems of notation. Let others sleepwalk. You are weightless. For you, displaced, there is no theory of weightlessness. You are the transit and the transport, the unaccounted-for anomaly, the ordinary pleasure of a slipknot as it slips. If you still had hands, what friction, what fire you might rub up!

Exposures

Such a small matter—a grit that chafes, a kernel that rubs at the core, at the crux—this late thought as immaterial light leaves the room, as viscous dark backfills the ambiguous space. Sleep is elusive. You wait for its moment of scission to set you adrift—a sublunar figure, a weightless aura, a water-edged contour, an emptied hull as it begins to sink.

: :

In the night of a long exposure, the moving figure disappears: not even a blur of ghost flesh or wisp of mist unfurled remains. Looked at long enough, the body in motion transmutes to plasma, to ether, then at last to the invisible. The body exposed is erased, a figure no longer figured.

Onlookers at the Scene

We should forgive the film its flaws. The rear projection—an unscrolled backdrop—bunches and sags. We should find solace in the painted hills darkling in the distance. Every hundred yards or so a streetlight rolls bright over the hood and the windshield. The driver keeps driving as if the plot were suspended: pre-dawn, or late dusk, sky-edges bruised blue. No one is in a hurry to see the trunk's cargo. We get used to the habits of time: the drag of the moment or the hour hollow, ice-encased. A door about to open, then opening. The weight of grace upon us, perhaps, in the endlessly-seized-after, never-held *now*. The void is voided, after all, by dark matter.

It's hard not to feel implicated in the violence that preceded this scene, the free tickets notwithstanding. The body broken and easily bent to fit the confined space, the look of dispassion on the driver's eyes in the rearview. We face the screen and see it for what it is: a limit, a barrier, a veil, a curtain, and a threshold. Although invited, we do not enter, are not meant to enter: the passage obstructed. At first sight, the body is all glare, a chalky expanse, and only as the camera dollies back do we see the curve of the hip, the sharp angle of elbow, the awkward pose.

We might as well be extras, onlookers at the scene, or mourners in Rogier van der Weyden's "Descent from the Cross," where the collapsed perspective engenders a feeling of unease. The space—illogical, cramped—holds more than it ought: ten adorned figures, a skull and femur, a cross and ladder. The tragedy—hemmed-in, constrained—is somehow manageable. The curve of the swooning Virgin's body parallels her lowered son's: loose, lanky, breathless. A bent weight to prop and bear. As yet to be secreted away. Sheltered. Sequestered.

How strange (*strange* as in: *from elsewhere, foreign, alien, external, from without, separate*) things are once we turn our attention to them, each thing bristling with the enigma of metamorphosis—mutable, unfixed, a shimmer of grainy light giving shape to a figure we can't quite place: a suspect, say, in a line-up, in what the BBC cop shows call an *identity parade,* as if some passing spectacle meant only for a carnival: as if out of trauma, one might tranquilly recall or call up the face of the assailant or the assaulted, assuming one saw either at such a distance and in such ill-lit conditions.

Yet we have come forward. By some coincidence, we were there the day the woman went missing, loading our groceries into the station wagon, picking up dry cleaning in the same strip of shops, and perhaps witnessed something suspicious, something seemingly innocuous at the time, but now, given what we know, out of the ordinary. The tall man, third from the left, looks familiar, but is it a resemblance and not recognition? Is he the suspect or a foil put there to resemble the suspect in order to test the veracity of our testimony, the firsthand account we have practiced and rehearsed, because what else could we do, sitting and waiting all morning on a bench at the precinct, good citizens, each of us?

The Closet

To illuminate a closet, pull a string. The room lit is even smaller than you had imagined. The door has a habit of coming unlatched. Maybe it is the forced dry air of the furnace or that the house is settling. If all the closet's clutter were removed, there is still no space for someone to hide. The door clicks and swings open. You cross the cold room and shut the door. Just as you are about to fall back asleep the door clicks and swings open.

Core Samples

The near pine and the far pine and in between the song of weather. How does one tether a river, or exchange the north star for a handful of pyrite? How does one draw conclusions, or with a rough cord and withy set a snare?

: :

To merge two gods into a single body set them upon a pyre. That which was not before appears as a compound, as an amalgam. As if from random words, a never-uttered sentence rises out of silence, an entity unthought of, unmade by the first erstwhile creation.

: :

Soon, a nimbus of stars will crown the woods. Soon, the woods will hold the stars aloft. At the cusp of another night: cobra lilies bow their heads. What is the tensile strength of light, starlight made matter on a torn web?

: :

I forgot that it was Sunday, that autumn is prelude to winter. I gave a beggar a dollar and he blessed me. I gave another beggar five dollars and she blessed me. Just what is the market value of a blessing these days? I could approach the problem, like a palindrome, either way.

The Change

Consider the unanticipated change not found among the sixty-four hexagrams in *The I Ching,* how now considering it, you are unprepared, stalled on a causeway between islands. All those years of direct observation, of darning and mending, eeking a little more use out of the given and still you have come up short. No adjustment of means, no filling up the open cage of the shopping cart will help. Above, the sky is like a baroque study of clouds, but who could imagine a single drop seeping from the silverpoint edge? The distance is a vast mire, but up close it's hard not to comment upon the tidiness, the orderly arrangement. An unexpected bouyancy explains part of the change, as if gravity were tidal and the tide just now turned. Sky and sea— not a single peaked wave. The water more dense in its salinity, but no less clear, no less inviting.

The Mystery of the Ordinary

Lace—frayed, torn, and mildewed—frames the boarded-up windows' sogged plywood. With gravity's assistance, loose wallpaper exfoliates. Hard edges slump. The ceiling distends. The crazed plaster softens into a delta of mold. The interior is the interior of a cocoon. The enclosed collapses, transmutes.

: :

A stranded boat waits for the tide, bright sun having transformed the craft into a glare of triangular luminosity. Often things are not as they should be—inside out or upside down—as today, when the tide stalled, it seemed further out, revealing a depth that had remained buried and unseen. I did not note it then, but only now, thinking about the boat high up on the sand that waits for the tide to un-tilt it and lift it upright.

: :

The daymoon's sickle is losing its edge. The scattered clouds are uneven spackle. The angels exempt from gravity lift like white smoke on a windless day—a radiant density without weight. The chapel is closed, under restoration. The unfinished work remains unfinished. On the stone mullions and traceries of the unglazed rose window, a pair of mourning doves roosts.

V.

Awaiting Election Day

Summer has vanished. Gray light slumps upon a bleached field of coral gravel. On the shore, a crowd gathers, pitches in to debeach a pleasure boat run aground. A man sifts through what remains of a burnt house, drops salvaged nails into a bucket. He hums a patriotic tune he learned in school. A home such as this, he knows, is embued with memories but this is not his home. The crowd shouts and waves as the boat sets off. Chained to a charred porch rail, a bike rusts. The scavenger is sure the owners won't miss the nails.

After the Yard Sale Before the Parade

Clothespins bob along a slack line. A 1954 Seeburg Model R Juke-box is a surprising find at the yard sale but she settles for another beehive glass insulator for the kitchen window's ledge. The part he doesn't like about a parade is the getting there early for a good view; the snowcone, already a sticky mess, drips from the paper cone's tip. His in-laws have attended the parade every year for the last five years. Why, he wonders, does he chafe so when her mother calls it *a tradition?*

Minor Arcana

Take away the constellation's name and one can imagine the repeated casting gesture of a sower's arm. The fall of each star random, inevitable.

: :

The thieving magpie offers as a curtain call the ho-hum and humdrum, the bruise of a kiss. Encore? The usher, impatient, looks at her watch.

: :

The only music for the quarantined plague doctor in his bird mask is the shivery note a finger circles on a wine glass rim.

: :

Only a dollar for three tries, but the games at the carnival are fixed. When the key is turned, the locked door of the fire exit opens onto fire.

: :

A boat on fire sinks into the reflection of its flames. Loose strands of web woven from light lift away through the oculus.

The Swineherd

Mark 5:1-13

If a householder, keeping wolves away, sets out poison, and inadvertently kills or injures a shepherd's flock, or makes sick some curious child, what judge would not demand recompense? These conjurers and magicians! Are they not responsible for their tricks, for the hungry spirits they let loose? And what about my neighbor, the bedeviled man who hosted a legion of demons? Who now will offer him alms? Who will not give instead to the blind widow, to the legless wheelwright, or to the pushy, pocked-marked orphan now that the poor man has nothing to distinguish his suffering from the others'?

The Angel Gabriel Bathing
in the Euphrates

Water and air are clear, tinctured by reflection, and reflection, no
surface effect, embodies depth like a flame captured in crystal, a
flame restored to *initial-ness*, to the *always* foreseen in the *now*. A
creek feeds a stream, a stream a river. Do the rivers of Paradise empty
into a sea, or do they circulate endlessly refreshed by movement?
All greenness comes to withering, yet look at the verdigris on the
angel's wings—the gold, the liquid silver, the mother of pearl— as
the wings stir the river, move the current, encircling the overgrown
edges of Eden.

Midsummer's Eve

Smoke spirals up out of the flames with the illusion of weightlessness, spreading itself thin, and dispersing. One can barely recall the catastrophe: the unseaworthy rafts at sea; the schoolgirls kidnapped, ransomed, but not set free; the cholera and famine; the city liberated as rubble and ruin.

A bonfire at midsummer hypnotizes. In its presence, one wishes to be no wiser.

Romantic Landscape with the
Garden of Gethsemane

Enrobed in shadows, the woods invite one to tarry.

If given an exploded view, one might behold unquantifiable dark matter, a graphite underdrawing bled through, the trees rearranged, composed, variants of the present site resited: a tangled screen of vine and tendrils, a distorted perspective to undermine the *reality* of the pictorial space.

The ostensible subject of the scene—look, Judas is one of the torch-bearers among the authorities— is overwhelmed by the fall of moon-light on leaves, what looks like crisp crosshatchings of chalk.

One might note as well the menacing fecundity, the weedy hardiness upon the inhospitable soil.

The receding depths are more forest than copse; the ruched waterfall is a diffuse blur.

A startled stag turns toward the viewer.

Still Lit

The three dead men aloft upon a ruthless technology are already in
paradise. The ones who strapped them up envy their weightlessness,
the way as the sun goes down, the three, still lit, hover like hawks
above their prey.

The Open Gate

My father left the gate open through which bad luck entered. Moonlight weighed on ice-burdened trees. A horse, ankle-deep in snow, lifted its head as a benediction.

When swallows trace curves and ellipses, when the horse gnaws at sweet grass, my father will return again with a gift of thistle, with the gift of a needle threaded with silk. He will return to find the gate open and bad luck like an unfed hound to greet him.

The School Nurse

He could see the nurse outside, a last breath of smoke released before she returned to her station to find him again, his third stomachache this week, after months of stomachaches. She shook down the mercury and without a word, placed the thermometer under his tongue. Twin silver-lidded glass canisters held tongue depressors and cotton-tipped sticks. Beyond the acrid trace of alcohol on the thermometer, he detected starch on the pillowcase, a waft of Pine-sol from the linoleum and sink, and the wiry scent of dried hairspray mixed, of course, with tobacco. When she smiled, a waxy bit of lipstick smudged the white of one front tooth. When she saw him stare, she turned to the mirror and wiped the tooth clean with a tissue. She straightened the folded white cardboard hat that designated her as a nurse. The boy worried he might die or get well and thus, their courtship, long unacknowledged as chivalry requires, would come, at last, to an end.

About His Past Lives

The man says, "I wouldn't call it memory. It's more like when you're at the movies, and you recognize a street in the film. You've driven by it—the Peruvian chicken stand, the mural—a thousand times—but the catch is you've never been to Detroit or Des Moines or wherever the movie was filmed. At work I'll be spot-welding some wrought iron—a railing, say, for a front stoop, something nice, Rustoleumed a flat black to give the place a Spanish feel—then somehow I have a tuxedo on and, seated at a piano, I play. I have never taken a lesson. By the cars driving by, it's the late forties, and my boss, this American, nods at me, like he likes the tune. *You take care of those hands,* he says. I don't understand him because this Havana and I don't speak English. In the past, that's about all the fame I have—playing for tips in a nightclub the mob runs. In another past, I dig for coal. Mend nets all evening by just a spit of candle light. In one life, I'm a mute, so I can't go on like I do. Who can remember being born again and again? Or what's wrapped in wax paper in the lunch box? But then I recall crawling out alive after an earthquake. Fire running wild. I help dig out my next-door neighbor. As a *thank you,* she screams at me, *Where's my dog? Where is Fido?* I think *Fido! Who names a dog Fido?* But what did I do all the rest of that day? Walked up and down the hills of San Francisco calling out *Fido! Here boy!*"

An Errant Absence

No specific order. Perhaps vestiges of a pattern to suggest material change over time. The planets align or at least from where we stand seem to. Perception is as malleable as time, as a dull soft metal that bends to the touch. The shifts in frequency suggest interference, an errant absence attracting, torquing, luring all the light into its vortex. Will we reach it: that moment when all that is moving away will cease before it begins in earnest to collapse together?

Negative Latitudes

Lit by the black sun's prime matter, the spirits of the dead, without intentions or destination, absorb the darkness. Still, the habits of the lost body endure. Given a map one carries it, unfolds it, consults it, although at these negative latitudes it proves useless.

The Arrival

The blown tattered flags point to the east. The black smoke from the stack of the west-bound train stalls above a brick wall, although it's easily mistaken for a storm cloud. The train departs; the weather is yet to arrive. The statue, with its back to us, looks into the same distance, shoulders hunched as if to cold wind. Or has the weather departed and the train arrived? Evening, certainly. Long shadows at acute angles to their objects, pointing east, or more precisely, a little northeast. We are new to the country and have not quite found our bearings. No matter. We leave tonight: beyond the wall, between the twin palm trees, to a further set of tracks. Our papers are in order and rattle now in our grips.

Valley of the Shadow

I say these words to arouse a ghost, some hoax, or hocus-pocus. The grid over the picture plane, the plumb line's veracity, the zero interest on borrowed time are what I have to offer, and as a bonus: the pale light of a northern sun, a dim lamp to depict and deceive, to mute the shadows. You have known all along that any resemblance to real persons living or dead is purely coincidental, just as you know, despite evidence to the contrary, that the *out-there* is less a vanishing point than it is a pivot point. For you, I have pegged off and fenced in with string a square yard of turf and recorded what comes and goes daily. I call it a paradise, an oasis, a dwelling place.

The Line Starts Here

The path, strewn with mulberries, ends at the sky—gray-tinted, cornflower blue. Night seeps in at the edges like water filling a scuttled boat. There is nothing I want to set straight. Like a spirit level's off-center bubble: the moon.

VI.

Opus Posthumous

Instead of a stone, a beehive marks my grave: white, stark, all thrum. I wait, weigh the pollen weight of dreams, on this less than comfortable bed of clay.

A hard husk, a thin splinter, I won't work my way to the surface by May Day.

Bees come and go as per their nature.

I hear the oak roots drink of limestone, hear the pill bug's heedless rush, hear ground water as it seeks and finds its own level.

If I concentrate I can recall the overgrown path that lead me here, the starlight: a thousand arrows—bristling flames—lodged in the hull of an empty boat.

What else can I remember?

A scum of kerosene on a creek's backwater.

When I turned back to catch the door before it slammed, I saw a dew bright web patching the torn screen.

Acknowledgments

Many of these poems, often in earlier drafts and with different titles, first found readers thanks to the gracious attention of the editors of the following journal. I offer deep gratitude to each of them.

Bear
To Fix an Image in Memory

Borderlands/Texas Poetry Review
A Story Coalescing

The Cimarron Review
The Late Shift

Concis
Ariadne on Naxos
The Return of Odysseus

Conjunctions
By Another Route

Diagram
False Sermon—True Story

Diode
Dipiction Without a Subject
Negative Latitudes

District Lit
Not Good with Faces
The Theft

Elsewhere
The Anvil

Field
The Arrival
Honeymoon at the Pine Crest Motor Hotel and Cabins

Foundry
Catalogue Raisonné

Gettysburg Review
Habitation

Gris-Gris
Romantic Landscape with the Garden of Gethsemane

I-70 Review
Exercise in Intuition

Kestrel
Awaiting Election Day

The Laurel Review
The Apprenticeship
Outtakes from *The Newlywed Game*
What Is the Purpose of Your Visit?

Miracle Monocle
The Line Starts Here

Natural Bridge
The Open Gate

Rhino
The Hyenas

The Southern Poetry Review
Convalescence

Sou'wester
Childhood

Spacecraftproject
Opus Posthumous

Tupelo Quarterly
Between Solon and Cedar Rapids on Highway One, 1984

Typo
Speed Dating

Ucity Review
After the Rapture
Prospero in Exile
The Sleeper

The Wallace Stevens Journal
Core Sample

Wildness
A Slipknot as It Slips
Last Sunday in Lent
Post-Diluvian

Many thanks to the graduate students over the years whose surprising writing prompts in my prose poetry seminar were the starting place for these poems.

About the Author

Eric Pankey is the author of thirteen previous collections of poetry, including most recently *Alias: Prose Poems. Dismantling the Angel* (2014) received the New Measure Poetry Prize. His work has been supported by fellowships from the Ingram Merrill Foundation, The National Endowment for the Arts, the Brown Foundation, and the John Simon Guggenheim Memorial Foundation. He is Professor of English and the Heritage Chair in Writing at George Mason University in Fairfax, Virginia, where he teaches in the MFA and BFA programs in Creative Writing.

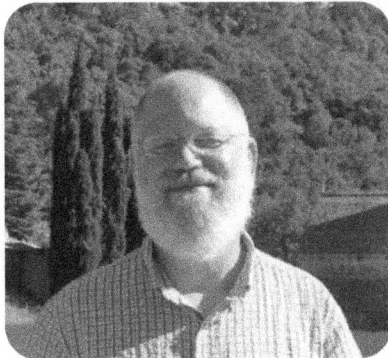

Photograph of Eric Pankey by a friendly tourist.

Free Verse Editions

Edited by Jon Thompson

Man Praying by Donald Platt
A Map of Faring by Peter Riley
The Miraculous Courageous by Josh Booton
Mirrorforms by Peter Kline
No Shape Bends the River So Long by Monica Berlin & Beth Marzoni
Not into the Blossoms and Not into the Air by Elizabeth Jacobson
Overyellow, by Nicolas Pesquès, translated by Cole Swensen
Physis by Nicolas Pesquès, translated by Cole Swensen
Pilgrimage Suites by Derek Gromadzki
Pilgrimly by Siobhán Scarry
Poems from above the Hill & Selected Work by Ashur Etwebi, translated
    by Brenda Hillman & Diallah Haidar
The Prison Poems by Miguel Hernández, translated by Michael Smith
Puppet Wardrobe by Daniel Tiffany
Quarry by Carolyn Guinzio
remanence by Boyer Rickel
Rumor by Elizabeth Robinson
Settlers by F. Daniel Rzicznek
Signs Following by Ger Killeen
Small Sillion by Joshua McKinney
Split the Crow by Sarah Sousa
Spine by Carolyn Guinzio
Spool by Matthew Cooperman
Summoned by Guillevic, trans. by Monique Chefdor & Stella Harvey
Sunshine Wound by L. S. Klatt
System and Population by Christopher Sindt
These Beautiful Limits by Thomas Lisk
They Who Saw the Deep by Geraldine Monk
The Thinking Eye by Jennifer Atkinson
This History That Just Happened by Hannah Craig
An Unchanging Blue: Selected Poems 1962–1975 by Rolf Dieter
    Brinkmann, translated by Mark Terrill
Under the Quick by Molly Bendall
Verge by Morgan Lucas Schuldt
The Wash by Adam Clay
We'll See by Georges Godeau, translated by Kathleen McGookey
What Stillness Illuminated by Yermiyahu Ahron Taub
Winter Journey [Viaggio d'inverno] by Attilio Bertolucci, translated by
    Nicholas Benson
Wonder Rooms by Allison Funk